Dress Made of Mice

Dress Made of Mice

poems
Sarah Messer

Black
Lawrence
Press

Black
Lawrence
Press

www.blacklawrence.com

Executive Editor: Diane Goettel
Book and cover design: Amy Freels
Cover art: "Ramping" by Jess Messer

Copyright © 2015 Sarah Messer
ISBN: 978-1-62557-924-9

Published 2015 by Black Lawrence Press.
Printed in the United States.

... in the distant past mice could speak. Their natural proximity to the earth's surface and their ability to burrow beneath it permitted mice to gain access to the ancestors, thus enabling them to foretell events.

—from "Art and Oracle," Metropolitan Museum of Art.

Did you hear me come in the door? It seems so strange to me that I may come here and write, stand beside you and you not be conscious of it.

—the discarnate spirit of Orman Herrick as recorded in spirit writing by a medium hired by his daughters, early 1900s. (Herrick Family papers, Schlesinger Library, Harvard University.)

Contents

III.

any beauty here is only because of t.k.—dedicated with devotion

I

Stump Speech

Never wear mouse skin. Don't point a mirror at the sun.
If you lose a tooth, crush it and throw it into the sky.
Never call rats or snakes by their names.

If a bear comes into your house in the morning, feed it milk.
To remove poison, drink from the egg of a vulture.

It's true I slept with Abe Lincoln.
I now know everything there is to know about this country.
Believe me, I carry a tapeworm for you the size of Kentucky.

When I walk uphill, I carry an arrow. If I can't
walk, I put a few donkey hairs in my shoe.

That black stone in my path is the iron house of hell.
I have always been kind to the black dog, whom I resemble more each day.

When I hear a cuckoo, I pray for happiness.
When my donkey brays, I say, "I believe you," three times.

This consoles the donkey.
When chased by wolves, I tie my shoes behind me.

If you want to find treasure at the end of the rainbow, cover yourself
in shit and ride a shit-covered dog.

You should offer, they say, your Cuisinart body each night to all beings.

I promise to give up this gigantic barge of sadness.
I will keep your secret my entire life.

Mouse Oracle

So afraid of death, you'd trust the mouse
with your future, marking which way
she weaves her nest, shucks seeds, arranges
plucked belly hair into a cushion for bright pink.
Each movement stacked with meaning, and you
are looking for signs.

This reveals a desperate side of things:
your roof is fixed yet rain comes in sideways
through windows in a room where someone
you love lies dying. You are afraid that you too
carry that sickness; your mouth, a basket
of cells, a basket left in the cellar
too long, growing roots and eyes.
                    Yesterday, a mouse
in the pantry chewed a tunnel straight through three
cereal boxes, moved dog kibble into shoes,
relocated navy beans into the utility drawer between
the duct tape and dull knives. A skittering, small-footed
undermining. Last night: a gnawing beside
your left ear—mice on the nightstand, unraveling
the doily. You yell anything: "hey you!" "oh god!"
but the army escapes with its thread-trail, a heart
with runaway arteries.

If you believe everything is connected,
then you believe in the prophecy of mice.
A mouse sealed in a pot of twigs might
do anything: strip, scatter, knit a roundness,

sleep or terrify, drop shits like ground missiles,
scratch its needles, jump, hide, bite.
                                    If you believe,
any of these things might happen: famine, wealth,
fire, flight. We cannot predict the future. The mouse
only rebukes the obvious: *look at your life*
more closely, watch how your pulse rushes
up and down your arm, how air escapes
your nostrils so easily. An unnoticed darting
in and out. One day the top will be lifted
from the pot, the shoe dropped from the box,
and you'll find a den of chewed airline tickets,
shredded pens, parka guts, secret magazine
collections, sandwich bags, the hem
of the old hammock.

At the center, a surprised mother will swiftly
paw the blind litter into her mouth
like wedding cake.

Marriage Proposal

Our love rhymes with: Cub Scout, trouble-shooter, sore
thumb. Sitting in the kitchen with our fruit cocktail skin.

Who says love can't last? A little syrupy, yes, a little soft;
a can of exploding snakes, yes, a dissolving Eros-aspirin. Yes,

I could be your silent auction—all that old lady furniture
delivered from the house on the hill: velvet drapes, china poodles,

chintz, chamber pots on your doorstep. Now & Forever, like
an interstate. Why not jackpot everything—imagine

those satin pockets in the dead ancestor's tuxedos. Imagine
the cool slide of your hand entering—imagine yourself dressing

before gilt mirrors, the wool seams unthreading, the smell of wet
sheep, and your hands moistening like pudding cake

on fine bone china—it isn't proper, but could you please
pass me that candelabra? I need to check the laundry in the basement.

Meanwhile, try to imagine a mansion of fabric against your skin.
Did I say forever? Yes, you'd better bury me beneath you, our hands

and feet tied. I want to be trapped by the cage of your ribs
as it slowly sinks into mine.

The Accidental Conception of the New Century

In basements with a square of shag, support beams, view of the furnace, a corduroy couch; in brake or bush without removing the corset; in the winter of gas-tax, and in the morning there was no one left in the trundle but him; the man whom I thought I had married, but all along it had been a fake; in the back of the limousine with glass unicorns and pink champagne; or in bachelor complexes that landscape with harrow and drag-teeth; window sills piled with pizza rinds, beer bottles like sentries; places I was not supposed to be; inside his cell delivering the tin bowl and rag; his mom out of town playing golf and we have the whole afternoon until the little sister returns from the Turtle Frolick; or our eventual confession of love for each other, the ribbon untied from my throat. "Come here for a minute. Come sit over here," patting the buffalo robe, the cold metal bleacher; my head a swirl of snow, hand brushing his trousers, the thought: I just want to be slanted sunlight passed beneath his door; I don't want to be a highway-bouquet, hair-jewelry kept in a box. I can be tiny and rattling inside as the room grows sloppy; his mouth too big, missing my mouth, my shirt and jeans in the crack between the waterbed and the wall; nothing but straw in my hair and the sound of distant musketry. My thought: he still has his tube socks on, naked and rising from the bed at 4:22 pm looking for condoms; "Maybe Dave has some," he says, about to walk down the hall to the port where a crowd is breaking bottles on the bow of the newest ship, and I think I will give him this present this once, as if I am the queen and he is the body of enlisted men, me with my powdered wig, wooden tooth, and Foxy Lady belt—I will give him this present, if he really wants it so bad, of myself. "Come back here," I say, "I can show you how."

My Life as a Puritan Bedpost

Felled from some long-armed forest, I knew nothing
of cross-cut or pit, two men pushing, pulling—knew
nothing of drag-teeth, November wind chained behind
the pointed rump of the horse hauling me
through vertical stands of my former self down
cascades of rotted leaves, and then carried
by streams and rivers, then barges and horse-carts, then split
by a circle into too many parts—but where did my
consciousness go? When did my leaf-line expire?
A split-beam bought by a Plymouth Furniture Company
at the end of a crooked alley. I became shapely,

bobbin-turned, yet plain enough and bought alone
for a jack-bed crossed to corners with ropes and filled
with bags of straw. Someone at last admired me—hung
their tawny camlet cloak, their doublet of dead-leaf color
over my head each night, wrapped me in their russet hose.
I dreamt the brazen serpent wound around my length, I dreamt
I wasn't a bit afraid, remembering Moses who lifted
a snake up in the wilderness; remembering snakes,
and smells and how occasionally I still thought
of rain. The clothes came off, were put back on.
Who could blame them? Weren't they charged
with breaking the images? With cutting down
the groves? I wasn't picky, and later wooden
stays replaced the ropes, and then a headboard as a part
of a simple wedding, then the curtains, canopy
for nuptial privacy, three more posts.

Then years lost rocking in some darkness, swollen
with salt. Then years carried on a flat raft up a river
stepped over again and again by mules. Then synched
and tied to a gunstock beam in some new homestead.
Standing for years in a wilderness inside the belly's cry
of wolves and coyotes. Then blackened by coal
in a rail-bed, a tenement; then blackened
by grief when the president died. Then reassembled
in another room. Moved again. Reassembled.
Given new stays and ropes.

Over the years, I creaked out of silence, singing with
heat and cold. This was my moment, more so
than a forest. Someone put their teeth on me, then
another dead hand. Fingers wet with birth or sexing.
I banged repeatedly against plaster, again and again
for every reason.

Now all the Puritans have died. But their ghosts keep trying
to lie down again and again inside me.

The Disincarnate Writes a Letter
Through the Portal of Your Body

The river opened a big book

of death for me,

              I wasn't expecting.

And now suddenly script, the spirit medium's handwriting,
blowing my body back into bluets.

Clock, cold, comb, cool—

                        a hand restrained

by memory and material: a girl, a glass, a glowworm.

I'm all these, now—scratch music and love
like a bore sack. And how surprised you came

to speak to me just now. I will try
to write more than just hot shot

and smoke, or longing for that
summer when the moon
hung like a talcum thumbprint.

Remember? Who has missed my terrible warmth?

My human life: museum of the worthless, shriven
and soured like a white dog
always running past your window.

                                                   All I am now—

petals of nothingness, vinegar sweat-flowers
darkening your shirt.

Interrogation of the Room's Unseen Presence

In whose name were you working these miracles? What part of you has died? Did you find any witnesses? Did the mob give any reason for seizing you? How have you astonished them? Who else saw your death? What became of the people who were cured? What vision? What wild honey? How long will your body remain dead? If a man says he repents but does not stop sinning, is that really repentance? Are you saying you are a new creature? What came to pass as you sat and ate meat with them? What was the name of the field? What does the word Satan mean to you? Deliver whom? What is this miracle called? How are you brought back? Why did he touch your clothes? What do you mean, wolves? Who came upon you? Who shone around you? Suppose a man gains the entire world, how long do you think should he keep it? What proof does history give of the wickedness of the human heart? Who came at last? What did the devils ask? What did you say to them? Has this miracle had any effect? If your soul is lost, how long will it be lost? As you gazed, who stood beside you?

The Spirit Medium Recounts Her Experience

Now that my pen is made of glass
I plan to write of this loud tree
and not simply fashion—blues and organdies
and other appurtenances—taffeta, pagoda sleeves.

Now that branches scratch the bowl of sky, leaves
massed loosely in torsade, flounces
deepening to knitted flowers, dead hair
braided into rings—a tree on fire with birds.

Nothing sounds like this loud tree—branches
have grown richer, louder still. Each bird like
a smoke-stained leaf, like mittens worn at meals.

Flocked with birds, the tree remains. Wings puff
and return like crinolines in wind.

Life now: delicate butterfly, a garnet made
of your own hair, parasols raised everywhere,
tasseled roots and ribbon ruches, sugar-lead,
bone dust, feather. Day and night, the sky
makes permanent the tree's singular pattern:

a dress burnt into skin. Now that this pen
is made of glass, I cannot measure
a sunbeam—I cannot catch a flame
with these lace fingers. Light darts from every
reflective surface like a velocity itself.

Branching, birds, and since you left: everything
I wear is made of glass.

Still, your image has reached my eye so gently
inside this light. Upon this slant
of sun cutting across this page. My body burning
for you like a tree.

Once philosophers tried to weigh a sunbeam, built
a machine so delicate, thinner than a fly's wing.
But the sunbeam left the sun more quickly, could not
be balanced on a scale. Love itself

is made of glass, is the burning tree. Ethereal lace,
brocade of all our seeing, weightless
yet still falling upon that sight, *belongingness*—

what is held by the beloved. What bright
light can be seen so clearly, unobstructed
like sunbeam passed through glass, or your
voice branching like the loudest tree, the place

where your hand lands so gently, then lifts off
before I even feel it. Like a thousand
                                    ruffles pulled

over my head, like a thousand birds.

The Man with a House on His Head

Once a stranger strode bareheaded through the forest. Soon there was torchlight, and between the dark torsos, he found a couple trying to dance down a tree. "What are you doing?" the stranger asked. "We are dancing down that raccoon." The raccoon's eyes shone down through branches, two green stars. The man and woman sunk up to their waists in mud. "Use your axe," the stranger said. And the tree fell like an exhaled breath. The raccoon, sensing his defeat, stepped out of his skin and handed it over. Naked, he covered himself with leaves and slunk away. In their gratitude, the man and the woman gave the pelt to the stranger. Silver and soft as the Milky Way, a fist full of goose feathers. "Now all the birds are safe," they said. Attaching the pelt to his waist, the stranger strode deeper into the forest. After sometime, he encountered a man carrying a giant house on his head. They stood face to face on the path. "I like your pelt," the man with house said. His voice passed through a crack in the door. "It shines like silver." "Yes," said the stranger, "Now all the birds are safe." The stranger could see the other man's eyes shining through the two windows, the crack in the door where his breath threaded out like smoke. "Would you consider a trade?" asked the man carrying the house. And because the stranger was a wanderer with no particular attachment to the pelt made of moonlight, he agreed. When the other man lifted the house off of his head, his face appeared small and distant as an animal. The pelt, when offered, was like a river in winter. The house was light as a basket.

The stranger strode off through the forest. He carried the house on his head, light and airy. And as he walked, he grew happier and happier, as if he were no longer a stranger. In the early hours of the morning he grew tired of walking. The man set the house down at the edge of a valley. Feeling sleepy, he opened the door and walked inside where he found a bed covered with white bearskins. He crawled beneath them and fell into a dreamless sleep. Who knows how long he slept, this wanderer? He had been traveling so long, his feet had become hard as claws, his arms roped from swinging. He slept the way a mountain sleeps, like the wind curled inside of a cloud, like an idea that does not yet exist. In the morning when he woke, he was surprised to find the house filled with food. Strands of sausages hung from the rafters, baskets of fruit, rounds of cheeses and bread spread before him, and as he sat up, the white bearskin blanket fell away, because it was the melting snow bank, and the food hanging from the rafters turned into bright red berries. The man's arms became wings that lifted him into the air. He'd become the partridge who, hibernating all winter beneath a bush, now flew out to greet the spring.

Rabid Dog

Finally, at the wedding reception,
he politely leaned over
and bit the waist of a neighbor.

She passed a tray of canapés, saying
"The best thing to do is take him
out behind the barn and shoot him!"
A stutter of laughter, then doom.
Her bangs flipping back like tidal waves.

After all, her husband was a stray dog—
in the yard he carried a mirror
on his back, his eyes flowering.
He spent his days in the city
snapping at bees, getting his nose stung.
In the evening, he returned
with mouthfuls of fur.

Truth is: she had been his wife
two hours when she chose
a new lover—what was his name?
(In the cramped dark fumbling,
smell of chlorine, an entire forest
of brooms falling.) When they were
through, a bare bulb exposed
the tiny room: he wore a beard, and
in the janitor's sink he washed
his hands over and over again
like a raccoon.

The Evolution of Rape Law

Knowing that at any moment she could turn
into a witch, they sit the girl in the corner by the fire.

They place a wooden cross in her mouth, cakes of salt, soap.
They place a coin over each doorway.

She says nothing. When they divide up her father's things
to pay for the scandal—his lathe, his axe, his pewter

bowls—she holds her mouth half-closed like a lock
that waits, a jagged outline, lizard or turtle, silhouette opening.

Either she'll lose her name or a neighbor will hang.
It is known that she has been with a man, in a brake or bush,

out in the land. They say she can change into a partridge or
deer, and that the night she appeared in a field

a man followed her. It's true when she moves, she makes
a shifting sound, and sand fills her shoes, filtering

onto the floor beneath her skirt where she sits still
as an hourglass. To try her case, they shave a bull's tail,

grease it, and thread it through her door-clate. She places
both feet on the threshold. If she holds the bull by the tail,

she can save her honor. If not, she will keep the grease
that clings to her hands. Her face shiny now like

warm meat. Years later she will still roll grease
from her arms. Truth will become the coyote that lurks

in snowfields of her eyes as she sits behind the invention
of glass, her thoughts crashed into again like birds.

Looking at Satan

Since his fall, Satan hasn't known who he is anymore. Simple truths have become hidden. Kissing women, he thinks: will they taste like fruit or meat? When he kisses men, their lips feel like bread crust, their skin like unwashed sheets. For my sisters, screwing high school boys in the boathouse became a habit. They enjoyed the deviance, their skin that smelled like mildew and lifejackets. If Satan was actually here on earth, he would certainly not be my poor father, retreating after the fact to walled cities, selling painted roosters as luck charms in golf resorts. He would certainly not be the man at the party who grabbed my hand saying softly, "This is difficult, but someone ought to tell you: in the past few months, you've gained a lot of weight." Looking at Satan, you can find no landing ground on his face; his left eye rolls towards the west wall, his nose slides into his cheek. He would certainly be a man, though; hairy, the way flies can be hairy, with tight iridescent skin like the flies that infect horses with bots. Death-defyingly handsome. And sickening. Appearing perhaps in the form of a long-lost uncle. So beautiful my sisters would collect the soda cans he slurped and the spoons he licked and make them into altars. They would shun the boathouse boys and practice kissing each other. So beautiful that my brothers would ground their speedboats on marshes, zoom their motorbikes off trails. At night they would dream of bending over backwards and falling into him like a pool, and wake up sweating. Even my father would devise transparent ways of keeping Satan up late in the parlor trying to grasp his mutable yet irresistible countenance. Only my mother would know the truth and not be fooled. Unfortunately, she would have had such a rich history of useless homilies that when she spoke the truth about Satan, no one would listen. Years later, when her ranting actually came from the voice of an old woman, she would finally be heard to say: "The devil's in this house, and he is using us to remind him of himself." Then she would take all the mirrors down and bury them in the back field.

Poisoned Mouse

The mouse just a comma beside
the woven wastebasket of the upstairs bathroom—
small, grey field mouse not acting
too surprised, alive but not moving,

nose in paws, his needle tail stretched straight behind him.
Nothing but a pipe organ playing beneath a curtain of fur.

I have lived on this earth only minutes.
And within that, the sleepy mid-day mouse arises.
Some say that everything perceived

is only mind. My mind and the mouse like a screen door
closing when I lift him—feet: 1950s white wedding gloves,
tail: a straight velvet tie—and place him in the trashless can.

Outside, America tries to climb out of its hole and most
believe in a God who created everything
only ten thousand years ago.

The mouse tried to climb out of the basket but failed.
I threw a bathrobe over the top and carried
it to the weedy beds. Here ants carefully unpack a peony's

balled fist, here some flowers bloom like clouds
seen from a plane. How I long to leave this country.
I look down and the mouse hasn't moved. I could never
leave this country. Inside, under the sink, I find

the blue pellets of poison gleaming like sapphires in the dark.

II

Ghost of a Mouse

If you hear ringing in your ear, it's only
the bell of my voice tied to your back.
After I cut out the river there was nothing
left but the mountain and the song
I sang to the riverbed. AC roared
in the highway hotel with one twisted
hair thrown down in the sink. A river
seen by a bird. All night long the black
highway sang. The moon was a mouse
who slept at my feet while sirens rang
and rang. I built two temples inside my chest:
one for literature, one for police protection.
The mouse didn't move. I spoke your name
into my palm and placed it under my ear.
Down the dark canal, the moon scurried over
the mountain, into diminishing air, the tan
hotel bedspread. Color of an empty
riverbed, milkweed-pod fur. All that was needed
to make a nest. But even the thought
of you couldn't last. I lay my ear right there.

The Right Manner of Speaking

1. *The Vowel That Begins*

Who had the strength to tumble off the train?
Working glass with your hands until it wrinkled winter trees.

Or keys rattling in pockets—*whisper, tremolo, glottis*
stroke—the breath between the pause, or

a furnace in which bricks are baked,
incapable of being subdued. Your mouth,

the center of the star.

2. *Clearing the Throat*

Because you told me, and I wanted

to be told. It was a command, and I wanted
to be bound on the bed with Ace
bandages and red silk rope.
                                    Every inch
knotted and crossed
like a boat before
a storm, but stronger.

                    Your teeth left a perfect
circle on my thigh. All week long it was

a forest clearing
where deer crushed ferns.

3. Breath

Can be held in the mouth
as long as we wish.

And you'll notice that the voice
is successful and begins to suddenly
vanish. A blue-stringed
wind covering

the inner lining of sky.
As if by the aide of a hand-mirror
I look within the cavity
of your mouth—

I can't remember
where I left you last.

It's hard enough to count
the intervals between the shovel.
I hear the mice in the eaves
at night, I reach across the bed.

But not all feathered limbs
are made of wheat flour, are made of grass.

I swing and swing in the open bed.

The roof above our heads is the one
we would expect to find.

Listen, as one sound
moves around the projection
of another.

4. *Emphatic*

You left me tied
to the bed, starfish.
Your hand strung with clear
ribbons of me.
I would cut off my own
arm to get back to you, would
stick my arm between my
legs if it could grow back
gold, a gift for you.

5. *In a Familiar Tone*

When you hold your breath for a longer
or shorter time—a body of midnight
outside of the city, a single tone
of quickness on slowness that can't
be measured. Like taking one's self
away, like being away from a place.
You would hang a cowbell around
your neck like a trophy. The voice
sliding up or down in pitch on a word.
I am your gentlest one.

6. Addressing the Crowd

I was still sleeping on the abandoned grandstand

while lilac-scented history unfurled, the color
of victory bows.

And the train moving so slowly through the landscape, carrying the body
of the former President, as if it were one hundred and fifty years ago.

I would walk a thousand miles just to see your face.

7. A Confession

I begin inside
the eyeball of a cloud.

It is my job to be this distant.

My mouth like an oilcloth
filled with leaves.

What I say is different
from what I mean. And what I say

is something unseen—how
your mouth emerges
from trees, a moth

lifting from bark.

8. Proper Timing

I open the book of role-play,
call you at work, say, "I still

taste you in my beard." Here is
my lucky shoe, flat chaps,
horse's back, the shape
of a saddle left in sweat.

Perhaps—wet for days and
the rain coming in sideways
through the open rectangle of glass—
this is how we live.

What I am wearing:
soft ribbons, then a harness,
hooked, three fingers in.

When I give up loneliness
to become a character
I am pulled from myself.

9. Enunciation

And after that: farther out than the deepest water

                                      cattails and sticks,

when I'm near you my body's a burning forest edge,

a brushfire.

                    There is no way

to know your beauty. I rake every inch

of the forest when you are gone,

                              I carve your name again

into the long boats of my claws.

10. Listening for a Reply

The ring of butter I wore
on my finger, the crown of dandelions. It isn't far

between a taut string and the sound of snow, the house
of beeswax inside your chest. I placed your ring

on the window sill for light to pass through.

11. *As if Heard Through a Phonograph*

Sound travels through

the hollow tube
inside a wooden
                    box

See how a voice appears, drawn up

                    through this flowering

horn that widens and flares
into an unknown
room?

A morning glory only lasts

a day, closing
itself each night.

How many ways can your voice
travel through me?

Mouth
like a bell

that only rings
when you are inside me.

12. *A Plea*

Or is it more like the long dark hollow
of a string set camera?

Looking glasses are in no way the cause
of danger. Perhaps with the indifference
of a suspension bridge, I place a mirror
beneath your lips—come into my country and live.

Resuscitation of the Apparently Drowned

For you breathe now with your whole body beneath the water

For luminous bodies shine on us through that portion of heavens

For we can watch the moon turning her dark side towards earth

For a luminous body is one that shines by its own light

For transparent bodies admit the light to pass through them

For I walk away from the flickering candle the size of diminishing luck

For I have noticed that the shadow of my figure on the wall grows larger

For eventually all of us will watch someone we love die

For now I behold as if from a window the small space of the retina of the eye

For the flame of a candle resembles your body reflected in distance

For my mind is also this pond; I try to remember death

For your body is both larger and smaller as I try to remember

For I see the rays falling upon the mirror; I see sun shining through that house

For we only see objects because of the light rays traveling to reach our eyes

For glass can be a mirror reflecting mirror into eternity

For something invisible always compels the shadow of figures to recede

For your body may also become a house to be shined through

For rays proceed from bodies in all possible directions

Like a drop hitting a basin making a crown.

Recipe for a Smallpox Mask

We call the pustules, "beautiful flowers," as not to offend
the smallpox goddess who likes to infect the faces
of children. To trick her, we wear ugly masks.
And here, I can tell that you may survive by wearing
thin leather cut with holes for the eyes, nose,
and mouth, rubbed with ammonia and mercury, a little blue
ointment, held in place by threads, as you lay still
on the pillow for three days in the distinct kind, and five
in the running kind. If you survive, there will be no pitting,
no cheeks ravaged like a piebald dog, and we'll paint the walls
of your room red to keep demons from entering, and we'll build
a corner shrine filled with flowers and fruit and brass.
To be safe we'll pierce each pock with camel hair dipped
in lunar caustic, and when you survive, we will whitewash
the room, we'll carry the shrine and place it on a paper chair
on a paper boat, and burn it in the river. And if you don't
survive, we'll burn your room as it stands—mask, sheets, corner
shrine—to drive the demon, the goddess who tricked us, out.

Cicada

Seventeen years later, summer drowns again in the voices of insects.

Come back from the dead and write one more thing.

A red fox lying dead at the side of the road.

Come back in a dress made of living things.

Three pupae caught in a colander, finches fluttering from rain gutters.

Come back wearing all the words you once told me, your hands fluttering through grass.

A fire ant followed me onto the plane after you left. When they pulled up the sidewalk in front of my house, they found a colony of rats.

Come back and I'll lie down quietly inside of your cloud. Which is my crinoline of want. Which is the sash your arms once made around me.

For many months, I went to the lake and saw the white egret.

Come back and open your neckline.

The sky is sewn by pairs of wings. But what kind of stitch is a swarm?

Come back and unravel your wrist, which is the edge of a pond where an old mill stands still.

Even the band playing all day in the park cannot extinguish this buzzsaw of longing. Someone left a giant fluorescent light on humming in the entire sky.

What will I see when I can finally look inside you?

I have looked for you everywhere but found only the cicada's empty flight jacket fashioned like a brooch to the trunk of every tree.

Self Portrait Without the Body

If you tap on the dead lights is the sound yellow or frail? I mean you with the teeth and hair. With a pancreas and eyelids. With unburned skin. You with a set of functional genitals. With a palate and voice box. With unfettered blood. With a clotting factor. With the ability to see color, to see with the aide of two pieces of glass. You, right here, with an immune system. With wrists and hands. You with femurs and body fat. You with this sense of perception, this breathing in and out. You who understands cold and hot, seasons and weather. You who can refuse to understand. You who can refuse. You with locomotion, viability and your opinions. You with your stature, your wars. You with thinness. You with a cheekbone, an IQ, You who can chew. You with your reactions. Who can choose not to react. If you remove your arms, where are you? If you remove your beard? If you remove your fingers, where are you? Gone from the hand that grabbed you from that galaxy of black river. Now: moonflower seeds where your teeth used to be. Pavement where your teeth used to be. Stars and highway weeds. Salt and wind but not your body. Horses and rats but not your body. Wooden spoons and knives and lemons but not your body. I'd press warm bottles to the soles of your feet. I'd draw back the grass from your eyes, I'd touch any part of you I could touch, I'd cherish every thing that you once touched. But the mind is made of forgetting and forgotten, is shocked. Where are you now without the body? How can the world breathe without your body? But it lives on without your body. Everyone continues to breathe without your body. Bodies create more bodies without your body. The room stands still without your body. There is a stone, a story, a photo in place of your body. Nothing remains of your body.

III

Dress Made of Mice

When I first met you, I wore a dress made of mice—fell asleep
upon the ground and a thousand, more, crept toward me through the grass.

They laced their tails and fastened pink claws across my skin, an instant
stitching as I rose up. I wore a dress made of mice, one last sigh and then

their breathing gone, they left only their skin which fell now lighter
than a breeze against my thighs. How had I become

so naked? And lost my human clothes? And when had the snake come in?
Silent, stone-eyed, it never blinked in our new light, looked the same

from every side, which was not like us. We changed with every sigh,
the same as the grass we slept upon. Beneath the bodies of mice, at first

we saw no other bodies. When we stood up, we turned the color of the sky.
The dress of mice hung empty with its thousand skins fluttering ghost-grey

then white when each cloud passed, two thousand raindrop ears, four
thousand
tassel paws—and then the dress became the grey-green bark of trees

shiny beads of possibility, the paws of some pink blossoming.
We were very hard to find. When you reached out to touch me, you felt me

barely there. There is no harm in love, we said lying in each other's arms—
There is no harm in love. There is no harm, we said.

Bridge

Once I stood scared in the lamplight
I ate marsh-root on a dare

I jumped every day of that teenage summer
from the highway bridge

into the brown river of drowned cars

until one of us got a foot pierced
by a sunken antenna

and it grew suddenly dark

as we stood caught beneath the lamp bleeding
and the marsh didn't wave anymore, gone

in its muck-smelling distance
while one of us wrapped the foot

in a towel and towels turned into capes

as if music accompanied
the oncoming headlights, a stage

but the distance of telephones outwitted us
like the concept of kitchens or socks
or the possibility of telling

anyone what we'd done, drenched
by the on-coming traffic, though it was

nobody's fault. We held
only night in our mouths

blameless and compelled as the cars
someone had pushed there

on a much colder night filled with
8-track music or lies rusting
for seasons below marshes

and bodies that still roared past
over the river, the bridge, past our bodies

wrapped in nothing I once lived in
a house, I thought, once I was

warm what kind of place was this?
Pushing car after car into brown water
and leaving and telling no one

yet everyone knowing anyway

which was why we jumped—
we thought we might touch it—
hoods pushed, left broken in muck

by distant adults, we might touch it
and feel something they did—push off
back up through brown water above

our heads moths flocked the lamplight
and bats with bigger wings swooped
in and caught them.

Vacationing in the Fur Trade District

The question was authenticity: silver Indian
bracelet, turquoise beads. You said, "Sterling,
925." I said, "Nickel, cannot find the stamp,"
and we left the pawnshop's dim arcade, your face
transparent before watches in the window's glass.

On Queen's West: leather jackets in a store called
"Skin and Bone," jeweled phoenixes that rose
straight from my high school feathered roach-clip
days. Parallel wall mirrors sent soapstone beavers
and rawhide drums off in rows.

You wanted one small drop of blue for your
right ear. The cost: splitting a pair. An infant
squawked and sucked a fist in the back room,
his mother stitching moose skin, surrounded
by fur. You said: "My old lover would like this,

she collected pelts." I looked at the tied
feet and noses—bear, bobcat, minx,
deer, cow. Twenty skunk tails in a barrel.
I thought of zoophilia: woman who married
a bear, a frog, a swan, who fed a cobra milk
and then fell in love. Or the man who married
a horse, a goat, a bird he held to his chest
and carried everywhere. I thought of each pelt
as you, your skin. Remembered the man
who stoned two dogs to death and hung them
in a tree. His only cure: to marry the dog's

sister in an elaborate ceremony, a feast
for a thousand guests. I thought about
the difference, a dog in a white dress.

That night you worried about my carrying on—
crying, raccoon eyes, my leaps between our hotel beds then
catatonia, unable to sleep in that tower of 500 rooms,
all with the same portrait above the bed—a naked
beauty cavorting against a furred beast; he a psychedelic
square of hair, she, S-shaped, pale, sleek. I prayed
our marriage would ward off bad omens, dreamt
of cages, stroked your hair. I couldn't tell whose skin
was whose. I dreamed I was your animal. *Let me
be your animal.* But then I woke and found our bodies
hairless in the mollusk-colored room.

The Nature of Emptiness

Striped woods, stirred berries and spoon collapsing
into forehead light—this was my contemplation interrupted

by the bear. The bear, bouldering into my cabin as I stirred
dried berries at the stove. Standing on my hind legs stirring when

the bear entered, a wall of fur, standing on his hind legs. I was married
to this bear. And so my husband entered with his bearskin

cloak thrown over his eyes as his forehead touched mine, and
the forehead of the bear touched mine. And I saw

him for the first time. His forehead shined a flashlight into mine.
Luminous, even though I was shy and looking at the spoon.

The bear in his bearskin made the cabin collapse. And I was married
in his hair. Then an arm, a spoon reaching through me to the cabin

window where the striped woods collapsed and left me without
a bearskin of my own. I wore a striped mattress. The woods

were filled with them. The bear said: you call that a parka?
The bear said: lets strip this mattress down to particles and contemplate

that. Let's contemplate, said the bear, the idea of the mattress
in its smallest form. And beyond that, the bear said, let's imagine

that the mattress contemplators and the mattress itself
are empty. Lets imagine our imagining is empty. Are you

gonna eat that? said the bear, because if you're not, I'd love
to have it. Then what would there be? No mattress, no bear, no idea

of mattress, no idea of bear. No bear interrupting with his stomach
growling and reaching for the spoon. There'd only be

luminosity, said my husband, the flashlight in my head.

Excuse

I had rejected every soft-handed suitor, but then
one night: you with your mitts and sandpaper.

In the morning my mother found the salmon you left on the beach.
Then the seal, the basket of scallops. Like this each night for weeks.

She was anxious to meet you. She rose early to greet you
but saw only a bear lurching out of the waves. We were discovered.

You carried two whales in your paws and dropped them.
You turned into a rock. A supernatural being of the sea, that's what

I tell people now when they ask me about my black veil, my net
and stockings. You can still see the spot where he dropped the whales, I say,

you can still see the rock. It's become a national landmark.

America, the Hallelujah

According to thy word. Affliction is
a stormy deep. Again the day returns.
And there is, _____, a rest. Angels roll
the rock. Another day is past. Another

six days work. Another year. As the heart
with eager. Behold a stranger.
Brightest and best of bright. Brother,
thou art gone. Call me away. Flung

to the heedless. Forgive my folly.
From earliest dawn. From every
stormy. From Greenland's icy. Gently
glides the stream. Gently, O gently. Give

Glorious things. Had not a word. Happy
is he who. Happy the man whose. Hark!
what mean these. Hear what
the voice. How beautiful the sight. How

blest is every. How blest the man. How did
my heart. How precious is the—
                              I love the volume.
I'm but a stranger. I'm but a weary. I sing

the mighty. It's good to give. I waited meekly.
I would not live. Just as I am—
                              Let every creature.
Let us with joyful. Long as I live. My country

'tis of thee. My God, how endless. My never-
ceasing song. Nearer my God to thee. Now let me
make. O, come loud anthems. O, I could find.
O, for a shout. O, for a thousand. O happy

day that. O happy they who. See what a living.
Sing Hallelujah. So fades the lovely. Soft
be the gently. Softly they rest. So let our lips.

                              Soon as I heard.

The billows swell. The cloud hath filled.
The day is past. There is a land, a. There is
a land of. There is an hour. There is a stream.
There is a world. The voice of the free. The winter

is over. This is the word.
                              Tho' dark and stormy.
Through all the changing. Up to the fields.
We come with joyful. Welcome, delightful.

We sing the bright. When down our heads.
When I can read. When I can trust. When our
hearts are. When overwhelmed. Where shall the man.
Why is my heart. Ye boundless realms. Ye nations

of the.
                              Yes, my native land.
Ye sons of men, a. Ye sons of men, with.
Yes, there are joys. Yes, we trust the day.
Ye trembling captives.

After the Election

Moonlight slept quiet beneath the grandstand,

like flower petals, like highway snowstorms, like each thought
not of November or battlefields. My moping climbed

the Pegasus inside my chest which sped me to you
in this last century of petrol, with my socialism wanting.

I dropped an ocean in the penny. It was November. It was
lost. My wish slept beneath the Pegasus, quiet

as a petrol station or the monotony of socialism,
as if each lesson was not separate from the thought,

but from the ballot box. Like a snow globe of wanting.
Like wanting thoughts not to be octaves. Not free

of the ocean, but of the battlefield. Like a grandstand
sleeping in moonlight, its flower petal confetti, its metal

steps like ballot boxes, sleeping empty now
beneath a dropped ceiling of balloons.

Prayer from a Mouse

Dimensionless One, can you hear me?
Me with the moon ears, caught
in ice branches?

Beneath the sky's long house,
beneath the old snake tree,
I pray to see even a fragment
of you—
                    whiskers ticking

a deserted street,
a staircase leading
to the balcony
of your collarbone.

Beloved King of Stars, I cannot
contain my animal movements.

For you I stay like a mountain.
For you I stay like a straight pin.

But in the end, the body leaves us
its empty building.

Midnight petulant
as a root cellar. Wasps crawling
in sleeves. I sleep

with my tail over
my face, enflamed.

Oh Great Cataloguer
of Snow Leaves, I pray
that you may appear
and carry every piece
of my fur in your hands.

Dismembered Mouse

All that's left of the mouse: a sailor's knot
of pink guts and liver like a lima bean—
discovered, front porch steps. Half

a head glancing up to doorway, mouth
opening as if to speak. Look—
its needle teeth now cut nothing
new. The fur looks fake, the eyes
the rubbed blue ink of antique plates.

I have stepped out with my dogs
in a ratty bathrobe. Years ago
the planet breathed and scurried,
now the ozone wheezes, *no hope.*

And which part on the doorstep
now contains the mouse? Half a face
about to speak like Janus
in the doorway looking west
and east? Look at each
piece, you cannot find its mouse-ness.

The world has always been in pieces.
It falls apart and reforms
in the corner of each year.

Like dogs, my dogs strike out—
one to woods, protector; the other
after the cat, a new hope, an assassin.

American Sideshow

Barker:

Love in all Shapes! Visit my gallery
of Portraits. Wolf in Sheep's clothing or
the Biter (finally) Gets Bitten. Love's
labor lost. Love's many machinations.

Love's lenten lucubrations. Love's tentative
Lubrications. False alarm—or No One
there. Love in a labyrinth; the adventures
of My Day. A reminiscence of by-gone-times past

ten o'clock on a Cloudy Night. Travelers, notice
the Nag's Head on the heath. Step up and meet
the Ventriloquist, a man in the Wrong Box.

Dummy:

        I believe in America,
the voice thrown from the stage.

I will never betray you.
Eventually he told me

how an egg is filled. How feathers
are hollow, the particular service
of the eyelid. What gives

blood its motion, our fine, beautiful
eyes, our limbs arranged in a great order

like fingers of a hand kissed
in greeting. Dangling, eyes
roll to ceiling. See how

we are always evolving?

Has the soul any passion?
Are the soul and body connected?

The men from the Side Show saying,
don't ever talk to anyone
outside family.

The men in sharkskin
patting their brows, folding their teeth
in kerchiefs and staggering
into the next room.

Human Canon Ball:

Beloved, I should have
called you fire because
you are not allowed and cannot
last. Like fire reflected

in the flash inside the canon,
and the carnie standing at

the torn target that is the exact
shape of the empty

tent. You never pretended
to love me. And fire is the shape

of that. A body standing
at the edge of sight-line—
forgive me, I should have called

you back. You—standing
just outside the target, the canon's
dark flash. I should have

called out when my body
rose up, when I left.

Fortune-Teller:

By the flight of owls, crows, by books, cards,
tarot, by radio knob, the entrails of animals, by salt,
bark or apple-peelings, by water, yarrow-stalks, Y of
willow-branch, by finger movements, a dangling key,
by flour, dust or smoke, by lamp-wick soot, by
bird shit, by lightning, clouds or thunder, by freckles
and warts, by planchette, by the shape of an egg,
by clock face, by thrown ribbons, thrown earth, by
a dropped knife, by handwriting, crabs or mice.

Hidden Dolls House

Behind the wall, the dolls comply
a last-touched positioning—the way
I found them behind layers of paper, chipped
paint. The tallest lists in a corner
leg-split before another, skirt-less
on her head and grinning a Colonial
gash of red. The third leans her hair
into a cup. Bodies stuffed, their porcelain
limbs chink when I vacuum
the living room rug. I used to think
the sound was money sucked up, not
a hidden dolls house swallowed
by a larger house, by driveways, highways,
and the sky. After the fire (in which the mother
and daughter died) the larger house was
gentrified, the dolls house plastered, boarded
up. Look closely, you can still see thumb-
prints flushing the ivory cheeks and
forehead rested on the cup as if about
to sip or raise the whole head up when
the mother cried, *Help me lift this kettle
off the fire, daughter,* and the hired
man ran for water.

History is a Falling Room

Do you like this room—
curtains with checks and
apples—it's a new room new
country I have never
been here I am in
your country now
but this room suits
you it tells me
something—how old
is that chair—about
you the mark there
is the mark I told you
about my back
against the wall remember
I told you it happened in this
room in this country I feel
like a fraud sometimes
No it's OK it's a strange
room it happened a long
time ago all the furniture
has been rearranged
the wine-stained
rug thrown out
Did you love
her—it was complicated
Why don't you try
this chair it's better I
think I loved her
Where is the mark

I have a sharp
bone in my spine
Can I move
this chair if you
run your hand along
the wall you can
feel it a small dent
I think I did
love her perhaps
it was my elbow
that made the mark
or hers Yes we were
in a tipped chair
I'll move it now We
fell together against
the wall Soft plaster
mark what remains
Was she everything
to you This room has
changed everything
yes everything

Today

Today it looks like a radiant darkness within the body
and the sound of the mice in morning and evening

and how the machine of my mind is never silent
and how I pray for silence like a rain cloud

combed through branches. Or the sound of mice
moving in last year's grasses. How light reflected on water

becomes a wavering lamp. Or how the pond catches
and holds the moon and the mice sing to it

while you stand there beneath your umbrella
and there is no more weather in morning or evening

and there is no more machine of the mind. Only silence
for a moment and the sound of the mice not inside or outside

the rain, not inside or outside the dark body of branches.

Falling Asleep While Reading

Inside my chest a city is building. I have fallen asleep while reading.
Outwardly bird and glass habit, an airport inside, and the long story

of a hero walking to mountain caves, to a stupa where a blue-haired
woman cries "don't you recognize me?" I forget my place, forget who

I'm talking to. The hero remembers, places the woman's foot on his head,
says, "please forgive me" as he remembers standing in front of the stupa

circled by dogs. He realizes he's been dreaming. I lose my place. I forget
the hero's dream and walk the electric walkways of the terminal watching

a thousand atoms all with the face of the Buddha, all with your face.
We want to believe everything has its place. But this is a wrong way

of seeing. I forget who I'm talking to. There's a bird caught in the terminal,
its nest built of luggage scraps over gate 32A. Before the hero fell asleep,

he remembered the face of the blue-haired woman, who was someone else
entirely. He woke in a room filled with wind and birds, long tunnels

of light. I wake with hair thrown over my face, the dog jumping off
the empty bed. Someone has delivered the mail, a magazine with the faces

of poets lined like airplane windows. The hero wakes from his dream
and flies home on the wings of two white vultures. It will be twenty-one

years until he remembers the blue-haired woman again. Whole cities have passed between us. Thousands and thousands of dreams and faces.

I want to say forgive me, it's been twenty-one years since I've seen your face. I don't know my place any more. I need to talk to you.

Coyote Aubade

I don't remember the coyote
or how I woke here
not remembering my body
or the shape that your hand
left inside me. Desire
on the nightstand
like an empty claw
and the candle
reflected in the dark
glass behind the curtain.

And beyond that, the sound
of coyotes in the tree line,
enemies of the empty trees.

A flame always reflects
the edge of leaving—unreason,
an animal. Everything
always leaves.

But nothing ever really.
It's morning and a coyote
crouches in the meadow
grass, leaping,
hunting mice.

Directions for Lines That Will Remain Unfinished

Line to be sewn into a skirt hem
held in my mouth ever since the unraveling

Line beneath a bridge
for years without hope I stretched my arms into the river searching for you

Line to be sent to the cornfield
history is a hallway of leaves.

Line written for electric wires
your voice inside the no history, sitting still

Line for future people
inside the work, only my empty teeth

Line from Maharaj
presently you are in quietude. Is it on this side of sleep or on the other side?

Line that cannot be read because of its darkness
impossible walk under weight of honey
away from your hands that break me in half

Line addressing President Lincoln
when the handle and blade are gone, what remains
of your axe?

Line to be run over by a lawn mower
afraid of everything and to be of no use.

Line for a distant midnight dog-pack
because I can never speak it

Line to be sewn into a shirt collar
the streak of your finger across the hood of the car

Line for a stone growing old
a sunburst that lands inside a flower

Line written only with your mouth
desire is a trick ghost

Line for the garden weeds
slowly I am nearer to you

Line describing the better qualities of monsters
are we afraid of what we wished for?

Three lines written for bears
inside cells, water, trees, I am meaningless
darkness and light wind like breath on fur
I carry the circling cities inside me

Line for a leaf blown into the hair of the Master
seeing you, I want no other life

Line for a mouse
to die like that, held in your hands

Notes

1. Description of mouse divination techniques used in Baule society in eastern and central Côte d'Ivoire.

2. "Stump Speech" borrows from Tibetan Folklore.

3. "Interrogation of the Room's Unseen Presence" uses found material from *Union Questions on Select Portions of Scripture from the Old and New Testaments, Vol. 1 Containing the History of the Life of Jesus Christ,* American Sunday School Union, Philadelphia and New York, 1827.

4. "The Man with a House on His Head" is inspired by Wampanoag legend.

5. "The Evolution of Rape Law," is inspired by a note found in Henry Reed Stiles' *Bundling: Its Origin, Progress and Decline in America* (1871): *"Ancient Laws and Institutes of Wales,* etc., etc., printed by command of his late Majesty King William IV, under the direction of the commissioners on the Public Records of the Kingdom. MDCCCXLI. Folio. From page 369. – The Gwentian Code: *A woman of full age who goes with a man clandestinely, and taken by him to bush, or brake, or house, and after connection deserted; upon complaint made by her to her kindred, and to the courts, is to receive, for her chastity, a bull of three winters, having its tail well shaven and greased and then thrust through the door-clate; and then let the woman go into the house, the bull being outside, and let her plant her foot on the threshold, and let her take his tail in her hand, and let a man come on each side of the bull; and if she can hold the bull, let her take it for her "wynet-werth" (face-shame) and her chastity; and, if not, let her take what grease may adhere to her hands.*

6. "The Right Manner of Speaking" owes thanks to John Dillon. Some of the sections are revisions of exquisite corpse collaborations with John using found material from the following texts:

The Household Cyclopedia of Practical Receipts and Daily Wants, Alexander V. Hamilton, W.J. Holland & Co, Springfield, 1873

The Modern Business Speller, D.D. Mayne, principal of Minnesota State School of Agriculture. Lyons & Carnahan, New York, 1901

Conversations on Natural Philosophy in which The Elements of that Science are Familiarly Explained, and Adapted to the Comprehension of Young Pupils, Rev. J. L. Blake, A.M. Gould, Kendall & Lincoln, Boston, 1835

Elocution Simplified; with an Appendix on Lisping, Stammering, Stuttering and other Defects of Speech, Walter K. Forbes. Charles T. Dillingham, New York, 1877

Studies in Physiology Anatomy and Hygiene, James Edward Peabody, A.M. The MacMillan Company, New York, 1921.

7. "Resuscitation of the Apparently Drowned," uses found language from *Conversations on Natural Philosophy in which The Elements of that Science are Familiarly Explained, and Adapted to the Comprehension of Young Pupils,* Rev. J. L. Blake, A.M. Gould, Kendall & Lincoln, Boston, 1835.

8. "Recipe for a Smallpox Mask," is inspired in part by the real recipe to be found in *The Household Cyclopedia of Practical Receipts and Daily Wants,* Alexander V. Hamilton, W.J. Holland & Co, Springfield, 1873.

10. "Excuse" is based in part on the Tsimshian legend, "The Bear Who Married a Woman."

11. "America, the Hallelujah" is a found poem of the first lines of hymns from *The Hallelujah: A Book for the Service of Song in the House of the Lord; Containing Tunes, Chants and Anthems, both for the Choir and the Congregation,* Lowell Mason, Mus. Doc. New York. Published by Mason Brothers, 1854.

12. "American Side-Show" borrows from 19th century carnival broadsides and dime novels from the collection of the American Antiquarian Society.

13. "Today," was originally titled "Poem Beginning with a Line by Ikkyu," and borrows the second line from 14th century poet, Ikkyu Sojun's poem #123, "Regarding the Pagoda of National Teacher, Daito, After the Daitoku-ji Fire." Translated by Kidder Smith and Sarah Messer.

14. In "Directions for Lines that Remain Unfinished," "Line from Maharaj *presently you are in quietude. Is it on this side of sleep or on the other side?*" is from *I Am That* by Nirsagadatta Maharaj.

Acknowledgments

Thanks to the following journals and anthologies where these poems first appeared (and in earlier versions):

"Today" (under different title) — *Ploughshares*

"Directions for Lines That Will Remain Unfinished," "After the Election," and "Prayer from a Mouse" — *poets.org*

"My Life as a Puritan Bedpost" — *Michigan Quarterly Review*

"Poisoned Mouse," "Coyote Aubade," and "History is a Falling Room" — *Green Mountains Review*

"The Spirit Medium Recounts Her Experience" (under different title) — *The Fairytale Review*

"Marriage Proposal" — *Gulf Coast*

"Looking at Satan" and "Rabid Dog" — *Post Road*

"The Disincarnate Writes a Letter Through the Portal of Your Body," and "Resuscitation of the Apparently Drowned" — *Eleven Eleven*

"Stump Speech," and "Vacationing in the Fur Trade District" — *Guernica*

"Falling Asleep While Reading" — *Catch-Up*

"Ghost of a Mouse" and "The Accidental Conception of the New Century" (under different titles) — *Salt Hill*

"America, the Hallelujah" — *Indiana Review*

"The Nature of Emptiness" — *Radcliffe Quarterly*

"Hidden Dolls House"	*Burnside Review*
"American Sideshow," "The Evolution of Rape Law,"and "Excuse"	*Common-Place*
"Interrogation of the Room's Unseen Presence"	*Newfound Journal*

"Mouse Oracle," was first published in the anthology, *A Visit to the Gallery*, University of Michigan Press. Thanks to the Schlesinger Library and the Radcliffe Institute for Advanced Study, which provided support for the completion of many of these poems.

An earlier version of "Bridge" was originally published as the song, "Union Street Bridge" on the album, *Miracle Temple*, by Mount Moriah. Merge Records, February 26, 2013.

Many thanks also to the UNCW department of Creative Writing, White Lotus Farms, and One Pause Poetry. Thanks to Diane Goettel, Suzanne Wise, Mark Wunderlich, Chiori Miyagawa, Nick Flynn, Ray McDaniel, Michael White, Malena Morling, Rebecca Lee, Lavonne Adams, Jeremy Morris, Jess Messer, A. Van Jordan, Elizabeth McCracken, Allan Gurganus, Heather McIntire, Ryan Vanderhoof, Kidder Smith, B Love Davis, and Atsal Khandro for reading early drafts and being the container— very grateful. Thanks to my family and friends.

Thank you Traktung Yeshe Dorje, Ikkyu, Lorca, and Li Bo.

With deep gratitude to t.k, k, and s.t. for their great kindness, love, and wisdom. May all beings be happy.

For many years Sarah Messer taught in the MFA program at the University of North Carolina-Wilmington. Currently she runs One Pause Poetry (onepausepoetry.org) in Ann Arbor, Michigan and works at White Lotus Farms.